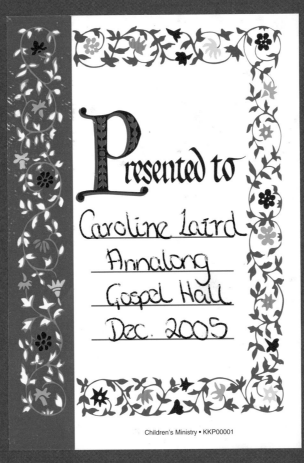

Presented to

Caroline Laird

Annalong

Gospel Hall

Dec. 2005

Children's Ministry • KKP00001

THE TRUE STORY OF

WRITTEN BY

Tom Dooley

ILLUSTRATED BY

Bill Looney

MB
Master
Books

Noah's Ark

First Printing: May 2003

Second Printing: September 2003

Third Printing: June 2004

Fourth Printing: January 2005

Illustrations by Bill Looney

Interior design by Bryan Miller

ISBN: 0-89051-388-0

Library of Congress Catalog Card Number: 2002116467

Printed in the United States of America

Acknowledgments

Let's be honest. Author acknowledgments are not usually intended for the reader. It's just a chance for the author to give credit to a few well-deserving people. Isaac Newton wrote, "If I have accomplished anything of value it is because I have stood upon the shoulders of giants." I owe a great debt of gratitude to all those who inspired me to create a new work on the story of Noah and the flood. Over the course of my research I read books, studied paintings, listened to tapes, watched numerous videos and even saw a wonderful musical stage production about Noah.

David Shibley, a dear friend and prolific author, introduced me to his publisher because he believed in my book so much and wanted to see it published. As a result Tim Dudley, president of New Leaf Press awarded us with our first publishing contract. He patiently walked us through the process while teaching us about strange new terms like, "deadline."

Wes Yoder, an agent who has represented some of the greatest names in Christian music and publishing is a dear and trusted friend of many years who took the time to guide us through the business relationship between writer and publisher.

Then there's Bill Looney whose amazing illustrations brought the vision to life. Our friendship goes back about 20 years. We're like two kids in a candy store, buddies who can't believe we get to do what we do. God always uses relationships to bring His dreams for us into reality. So, thank you, Lord, for your awesome and mysterious ways which are beyond finding out.

And finally, thanks to you, dear reader, who now hold this book in your hands. I pray it will bless you and fill you with fresh wonder for the God who made the Heavens and the Earth and who "makes all things new again."

This book encompasses one of the oldest events in the history of the world. It has been told and retold for

centuries and is not confined to one nation or culture. Nearly all people groups have a similar story in their history.

Because it has been mostly handed down from one generation to the next by word of mouth, it has varied somewhat

with each retelling, and has many different versions around the world. Therefore, to get an accurate account, we must

go to the original source where it was recorded at the outset in writing — the Bible.

Here, the account doesn't begin with "once upon a time," because it isn't a fable, a legend, or a Nobel prize-winning work of fiction. This true account begins with "in the beginning," and the next word, "God," verifies the Author and the veracity of the story. The creation does not need to be covered in detail here, but it should be understood that everything in the beginning was perfect. God's creation contained no flaws, no mistakes, no sin, and no death of animals or humans. The first man and woman were perfect — until temptation and sin corrupted them.

$\mathcal{T}$he Bible states that as man began to multiply on the earth, there were those who dwelled in tents and had

livestock (probably for clothing and not for eating, as man wasn't told he could eat meat until after the Flood).

Even with the curse that God had placed on the earth because of man's rebellion in the Garden, the world's first

farmers also probably raised some amazing crops in the soil God had created for the plants in which to grow. As

man multiplied, so did his interests, vocations, and talents. There were those who played music on the lyre and pipe.

There were those who forged implements of bronze and iron.

The Bible doesn't record much information about the world before the Flood, but the people of this time were very intelligent. Some began to build highly developed cities exemplifying the advanced intelligence of civilization at the time. Maybe there were great metropolises of thousands of people working together, living together, developing new ideas, and making great strides in the standards of living.

$\mathcal{M}$any scientists believe that in Noah's day the world was still dripping with the fresh glory of God's creative majesty. The beauty of that original Earth must have been astounding.

$\mathcal{B}$efore the Flood, the Bible records that people lived to be almost a thousand years old. The human gene pool, just recently created, was still relatively untainted by mutations and other problems resulting from sin and the curse, so presumably there would have been much less major sickness, or physical and mental handicaps. We can assume the people were fairly healthy and strong. A couple could potentially produce a large number of children over a thousand-year lifespan. Also, most likely these people were highly intelligent and very sophisticated.

Think about it. What could you learn and accomplish if you enjoyed great health and could live several hundred years? Who knows, but it's not beyond the realm of possibility for such people to have produced a civilization with some sort of sophisticated technology, libraries, theaters, museums and temples of worship.

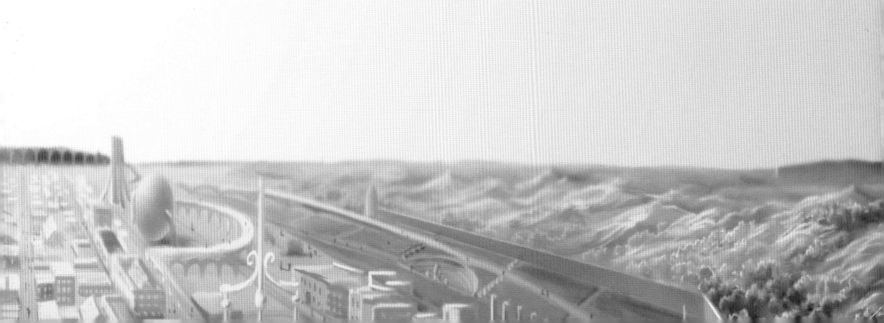

$\mathcal{H}$owever, regardless of the amount of knowledge that had accumulated, and to what extent their talents

and skills became sharper and more refined, the Bible records that the wickedness of these people grew to almost

unimaginable proportions. We are told that they were evil, violent, and totally corrupt. The Lord was very

grieved because of what man was doing. He warned that He would destroy the earth (including man, and the

land animals — beasts, flying creatures and every creeping thing) with a flood.

$\mathcal{H}$owever, there would be some special exceptions to this total destruction. Representatives of all the land

animals would be saved. Also, one man found grace in the eyes of the Lord. His name was Noah. God promised

this very special man that he and his family (including his wife, three sons and their wives) were to be saved from

this terrible judgment. These were the chosen ones, eight people chosen by God to be the seed of a new world. God explained to Noah what was about to happen — total destruction, the end of the earth as Noah knew it. God told Noah that he and his family had been chosen to begin life again on the other side of the Flood.

God instructed Noah to build an ark of safety that would not only protect his family through the coming deluge, but would also preserve a male and female of each kind of beast, flying creature, and creeping thing. God gave Noah explicit instructions on how to build the Ark and what to do. So with the help of his three sons, and possibly others, the great work began.

$\mathcal{T}$o build an ark of such proportions as the Lord had detailed must have seemed a formidable task to Noah. But not only had God given him three strong sons, He also promised to be with him every step of the way. The Lord would have made sure Noah was able to obtain everything he needed. Noah's faith was surely magnified daily as the Lord overcame every obstacle for him. But there was one thing Noah had never seen and could not even imagine what it would be like — a global flood.

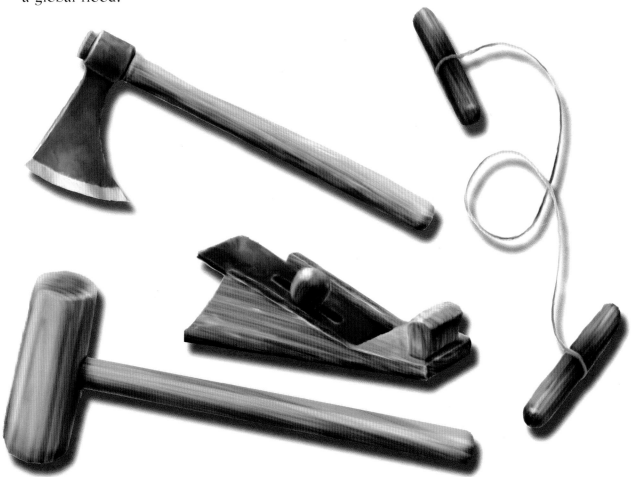

$\mathcal{B}$eing just a man, Noah's finite mind could not comprehend the whole globe covered by water. How could he convince people that such an event was about to happen? Presumably there was no evidence such a cataclysm was about to occur — just one man's word that God told him it would. When Noah spoke of it, some probably just stared

at him with a withering silence and disbelief. Some would openly scoff, calling him crazy, but God said it would happen, so there was no doubt in Noah's mind. He knew the day would soon come when God would cause water to rise upon the earth and destroy the civilization in which he lived.

Working on the ark was probably a daily routine for Noah. He likely spent many evenings discussing what such a Flood would do to the earth, or how much progress had been made that day, or the building plans for the next day. Perhaps his family played music and sang praises to God for the promise of salvation He had given them. Being a devout family, they undoubtedly worshiped God and thanked Him for seeing them safely through another day. Being

human, they probably experienced feelings of uncertainty from time to time as they pondered the enormity of all that lay before them.

The thought that the world around them would be completely destroyed, and that they would be the only survivors (if no one else believed God's warning through Noah — which sadly is what happened), must have been totally unfathomable.

During the long years of construction, Noah and his crew may have exhausted the wooded area nearest the Ark. Perhaps the men had to hike over the hill and down into the adjacent valley to gather timber. If so, the days certainly became harder than they used to be, but the work never ceased. Days turned into weeks; weeks turned into months; months turned into years. The project was nearing completion. Now, something else that had never been seen before started to happen.

Exactly how it happened we aren't told, but it may have been like this. Every day, new animals were coming to the areas near the construction site. There were big ones with fur or horns and smaller ones with long tails that did funny things. There were short ones with masks and long ones with stripes and beautiful birds of all kinds! All of these animals were gentle and Noah knew they had been sent to go on board the ark. "What a marvelous God to create such variety," Noah must have exclaimed.

"So many of them and all so magnificent!" Their number was growing each day so he knew the time was short. *I wonder if they'll all fit on the ark,* he probably thought to himself. *Of course they will. This is the Lord's plan.* So, we can picture Noah, there by a stream, in the silence of his heart, worshiping God.

$\mathcal{A}$fter the last timber had gone into place, it probably took the people quite some time to seal all of the joints in the shell of the Ark, but it was finally done. The construction part of the project was finished. Noah and his family very likely rejoiced and gave thanks to God. Somewhere along the way the great march began. If we had been there, perhaps we would have seen them begin to stir. Not just a few but all of them at once. It was like someone turned a switch and every animal that had come to the Ark responded at the same moment. It wasn't sudden — just deliberate.

They all stood up together and slowly began moving toward the ark. Surely Noah and his family marveled in amazement at the orderly procession.

$\mathcal{I}$n his heart, as Noah saw the people reject God's warning, he might have asked, "How can even the animals

know what man cannot comprehend?" Put yourself there and imagine: As far as the eye could see, they came. This

march was being orchestrated by God himself. The Great Conductor was leading a symphony of animals, calling to

each one in a voice only they could hear. And so they came. By the thousands they came.

It took a week to load and place all the animals. During this time, the family would have also been working diligently to gather all remaining provisions into the ark. There was certainly a sense of urgency as they hurried to prepare for something none of them could even begin to envision. God's instructions had been followed almost completely, but there was one detail left.

The door of the Ark had been open since it was built – perhaps for a number of years, a standing invitation for anyone

to enter in and be saved from the coming catastrophe. But no one outside of Noah's family came because no one believed.

Mercifully, the door was open during those last seven days, but what are seven days to years? The fact that the door was

still open didn't matter to the mocking crowds outside of the Ark. Finally, on the seventh day, God shut the door. This was

the day for which Noah had waited more than 100 years. He knew the great event was only moments away.

Now the anticipation was almost unbearable for the eight people about to embark on the greatest human adventure the world would ever know.

The noise level inside the ark must have been deafening as all the animals raised their voices in a great cacophony. The thought may have crossed Noah's mind that this could be their way of rejoicing over their deliverance from what was about to happen. The most amazing thing was that they were all able to fit on the ark with room to spare. It's possible Noah may have been concerned that some might be too large. However, even for the large dinosaurs, God most likely sent average-sized young adults.

If the earth were to be repopulated after the Flood, it would make sense for this to be accomplished by the young. The older fully-grown creatures would probably not adapt as well or as quickly as the young, nor would they last as long. Noah may even have thought of the youth and vigor of his own three sons and their wives. We can almost hear him thinking, *Yes, the future belongs to the young.* Many times, Noah surely marveled at the wisdom of God.

*I*n your mind, put yourself on the Ark. Let yourself dream a little. The noise level has dropped. The animals have grown quiet. Just a few days ago they had all stood up together and marched to the Ark. Now they were all lying down together and becoming still. They knew it was time. Instinctively everyone looked up and for a moment stood in breathless silence listening . . . waiting.

And from that time to now, every flood has had its beginning with one single drop of water.

$\mathcal{A}$ rumbling noise shakes the earth. Suddenly the fountains of the great deep burst open, erupting with such tremendous force that water and debris shoot high into the sky. Earthquakes break open huge cracks in the land. People begin running in all directions trying to escape the cataclysm. Volcanoes erupt, sending plumes of ash and rock into the sky and raining down fireballs for miles in all directions.

Based on the time spent in the Ark, as recorded in Genesis Chapters 6-9

The rain fell for 40 days	40
The waters of the Flood kept rising for an additional 110 days	110
The waters receded over the next 74 days (assuming 30 days to a month)	74
After another 40 days, Noah sent a raven out of the Ark	40
After another 7 days, Noah sent out a dove	7
After another 7 days, the dove was sent out for the second time	7
The third sending of the dove was after another 7 days	7
Another 29 days elapsed	29
57 days elapsed from when the covering of the Ark was removed to the final day	57
Total days in the ark	371

hen it starts to rain. The drops become a shower. The shower becomes a downpour. The downpour becomes a raging torrent, and the deluge comes upon the world — water from the sky above; water from the earth below.

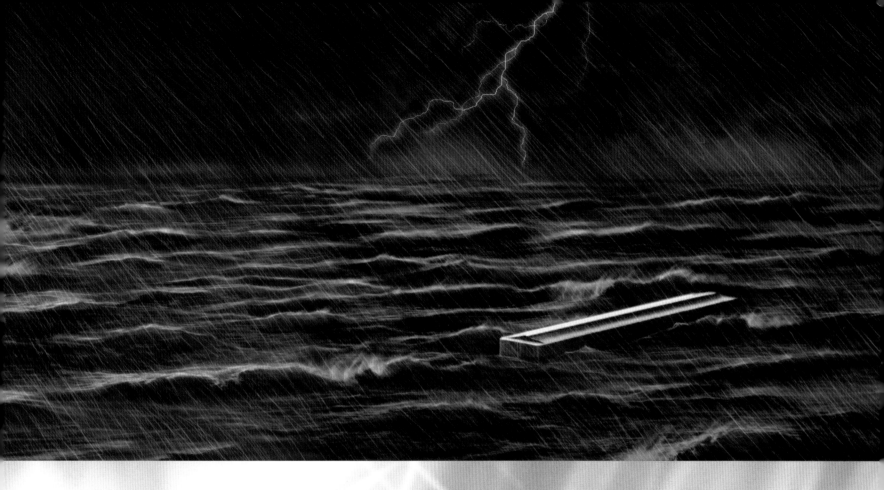

The thunderclaps and explosions and jarring vibrations continue for days. The Ark is tossed and spun and tipped and flung, but it never capsizes. The passengers on the Ark cling to one another and pray. The waters prevail and greatly increase on the earth, as the Ark begins to move about on the surface of the waters. The waters prevail exceedingly on the earth, and all the high hills under the whole heaven are covered. What a scene has been imagined — but it may well have been something very much like this.

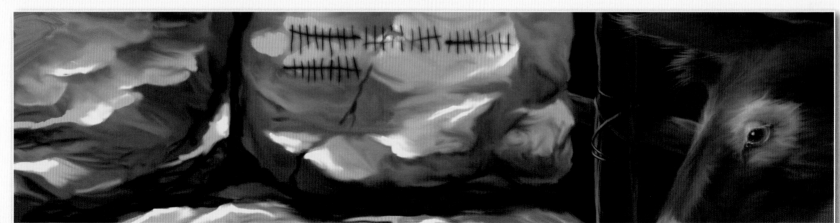

What was it like to be in Noah's shoes? What was life like aboard the Ark during the Flood? The Bible tells us very little about this time, so we can only speculate. After 40 days and nights of rain, thunder, cataclysmic noises, and endless rocking of the Ark, the 41st day arrived. Noah was barely asleep. He lay in a twilight kind of slumber, but it felt good to rest there in the quiet of the new day. *Wait a minute*, he thought. *Why is it so quiet?* The moment he opened his eyes he knew something was different.

The bewildered Noah arose and moved toward the light filtering in from above. He reached out for the ladder and began to climb. Some of the animals turned their attention to their master. He climbed to the highest level where the opening ran the length of the ark.

His eyes smarted from the brightness of the light, the glorious light. This glorious, wonderful light was the dawning of a new day . . . and a new world. The emotions of excitement, wonder, gratitude, and a sense of loss overwhelmed Noah at once. The rain had stopped.

*H*e covered his eyes, bowed his head and wept, thanking and praising God for His protection. Noah's eyes slowly adjusted to the light, and he looked out upon the endless sea in awe and wonder. As he gazed on the emptiness, he felt a deep sadness for the lost and beautiful world that was now gone forever — a world that God himself had created and called very good. That world would never again be seen by human eyes. Today marked the beginning of a new history.

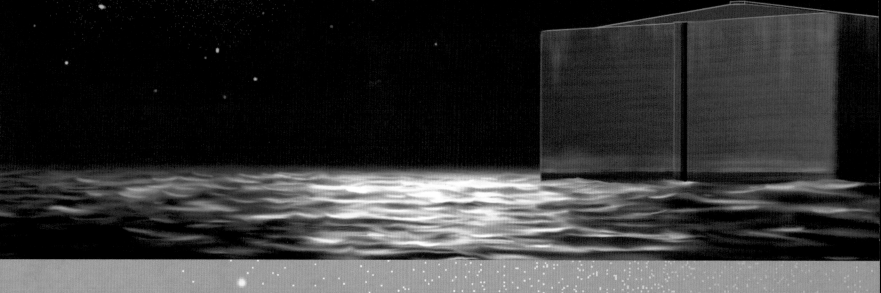

That night, the sky presented a wonderful spectacle. The lucid sky was so brilliantly lit with stars that they felt they could reach out and take hold of any one they pleased. They remained there, gazing at the stars, until well past their usual time of retiring. Few words were spoken.

*T*he days ahead were filled with activity as everyone adjusted to life aboard the ark. There was plenty of work

to do. Nobody was bored. Caring for the animals was a big job, but Noah and his family had little else to do except

take care of themselves and their precious cargo. God had prepared every animal for this preservation period, so

there were no predators attacking prey and no animals tried to escape from the ark. For this brief period, peace and

harmony reigned. There was probably no

sickness or death aboard the ark. Surely

the serenity was much like that which will be present in the new earth when it's restored.

$\mathcal{T}$he Bible records that from the time that God had shut the door of the ark until now had been about five

months. Such a long period of ark living must have been quite tiresome. No doubt Noah's family was thankful

for their safety and provisions; however, one could imagine them becoming restless, ready to get their feet on dry

land once again.

The waters were continually receding now, and the level was decreasing daily. One day there was much excitement on the Ark when suddenly a jolting vibration shook the great ship and everything in it. The Ark had landed! The great vessel had come to rest at the top of a mountain, but the land mass was still mostly hidden by the water. The Ark rested there as the water level continued to drop for three more months. Looking out from the Ark, Noah saw the tops of mountains that had been uplifted as part of the ending processes of the Flood. Although they must have been anxious to leave the Ark, Noah and his family continued to wait for the earth to dry and for God's timing. Finally, in the ninth month, Noah sent out two birds – a raven and a dove. The raven must have found something to scavenge, for it did not return. The dove, however, found no place suitable to land, and so returned to the Ark.

Noah sent the dove out again a week later, and the dove came back with an exciting find — an olive leaf was in its

mouth. This was good news for Noah and his family. It meant that they would soon be leaving the Ark. After one

more week passed, Noah let the dove go once more, and this time the dove did not return.

$\mathcal{F}$inally, the day came when God instructed Noah to leave the Ark. He told Noah to bring out his family and every living thing that was in the Ark. The ground was dry now, and having stayed in the Ark for over a year, this was certainly an exciting day for the eight people who had left one world behind, and were stepping out into a vast, new land.

The first thing that Noah did upon leaving the Ark was to build an altar and offer a sacrifice to God for His bountiful goodness and mercy. Extra numbers of clean animals had been brought on board the Ark just for this purpose. God promised Noah that He would never again destroy the world with water, and gave Noah a sign of His covenant — a rainbow. To this day, the rainbow is a reminder of the faithfulness of God and the obedience of a man wholly dedicated to God.

Although man was corrupt, God provided a way for life to be preserved in Noah's day through an Ark of Salvation. Today, God has provided another Ark of Salvation so people can be saved — the Lord Jesus Christ who died on a cross to pay the penalty for our sin, and was raised from the dead. Jesus said, "I am the door. If anyone enters by me, he will be saved" (John 10:9). The door is still open for all who will believe to enter.

A Closer Look

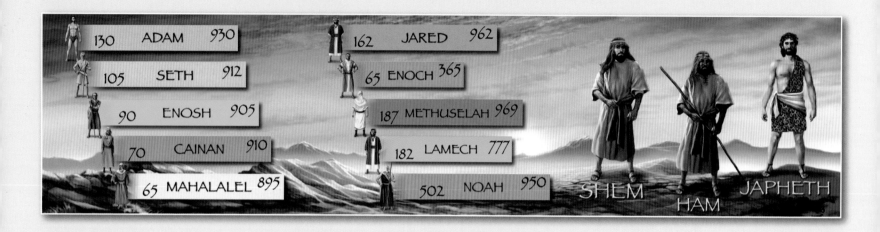

130 ADAM 930
105 SETH 912
90 ENOSH 905
70 CAINAN 910
65 MAHALALEL 895
162 JARED 962
65 ENOCH 365
187 METHUSELAH 969
182 LAMECH 777
502 NOAH 950
SHEM   HAM   JAPHETH

How much time passed between Adam and the Flood?

The time from the Creation to the time of the great Flood was only 1656 years. This can be calculated from the genealogy listed in Genesis 5. The chart above summarizes this genealogy. The number on the left represents the age of each man when his son (the name following his name) was born. The number on the right is each man's age when he died. For example, Adam was 130 when Seth was born, and he lived to be 930. If you add up the ages on the left, you get a total number of years of 1558 through the birth of Noah's first son, at which time Noah was 502 years old. Since Noah was 600 at the time of the Flood, add another 98 years to 1558, and you come to the total of 1656 years from Adam to the Flood.

What was the Ark really like?

First of all, it's an Ark. It's not a boat. That difference is very important. At right is the image most of us have of Noah's ark.

Look familiar? This kind of image has been used for so many years as a symbol of Noah and the Ark that most people have come to believe that this is what it actually looked like. The image most of us have of the Ark is that of a relatively

small boat with a little house in the middle and animals walking around on an outside deck. In fact, Noah's ark was perfectly designed by God for stability in rough seas. The Ark was six times longer than it was wide. Modern ocean-going vessels like aircraft carriers and oil tankers are still built to this same ratio. When it was fully loaded, the Ark displaced about 22 feet of water. Since it was 45 feet high, just about half of the Ark was submerged with the other half above the water line — the perfect ratio for stability in the water. In fact, it was one of the most stable floating platforms ever built. Even in a sea of gigantic waves, the Ark could be tilted through any angle to almost 90 degrees and still right itself. It's a cute symbol but, like most symbols, bears very little resemblance to the thing it represents.

The Hebrew word for "ark" does not mean "boat." It means, quite literally, "box." That's right — "box." Remember the Ark of the Covenant? It was a specially designed box that carried the Ten Commandments. So, the Hebrew word for ark is "box." There was no outside deck. Everybody and everything was contained inside the Ark. Remember this was not a boat.

Texas Stadium, Dallas, Texas

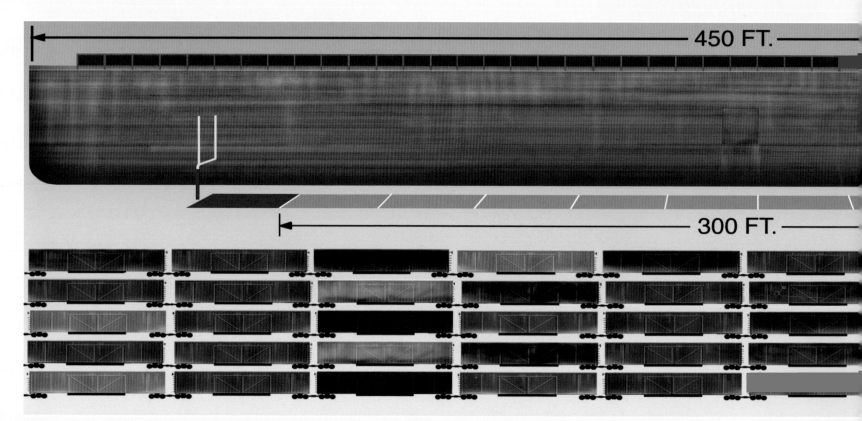

450 FT.

300 FT.

Boats are designed to go somewhere, to be propelled through the water under power. The Ark had no propulsion system. No engine, no sails, no rudder, nothing. It was the power of God that preserved the Ark as it floated on the water. All that the Ark was designed to do was stay afloat for one full year as a place of shelter and provision for the people and animals on board. The Ark was just a great big floating box. The Ark was approximately 450 feet long, 75 feet wide, and 45 feet high. It's hard to imagine just how big the Ark was until it is set alongside something else for comparison, which these illustrations show. A football field is 300 feet from end to end; the Ark was 150 feet

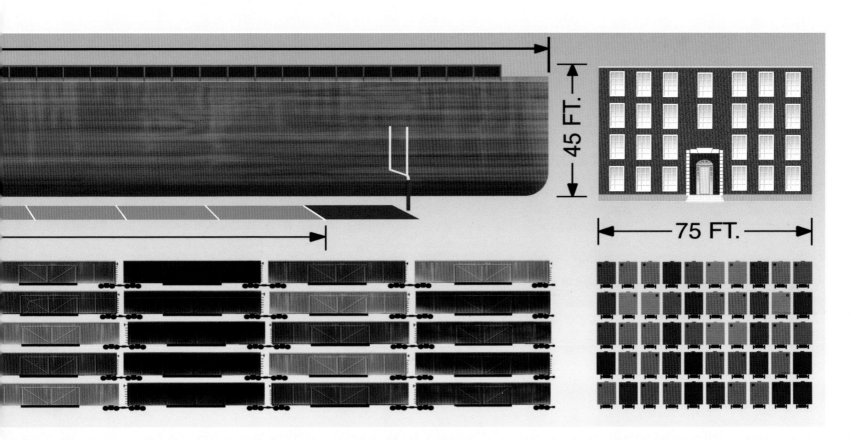

45 FT.

75 FT.

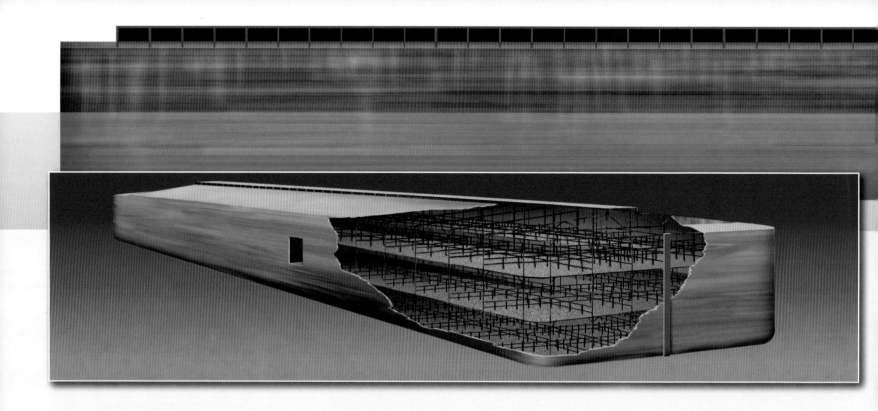

longer. It was as tall as a four–story building. Inside, the Ark had a cargo capacity equal to that of 522 standard railroad stock cars.

Each one of those railroad cars can hold 240 medium–sized animals. Only 188 of these railroad cars would be needed to hold 45,000 sheep–sized animals (many more than were needed to represent all the *kinds* of land animals). That would leave 334 railroad cars for food, water, a huge aviary for the birds, plenty of living space for Noah's family, and some "range area" for any of the animals to walk around.

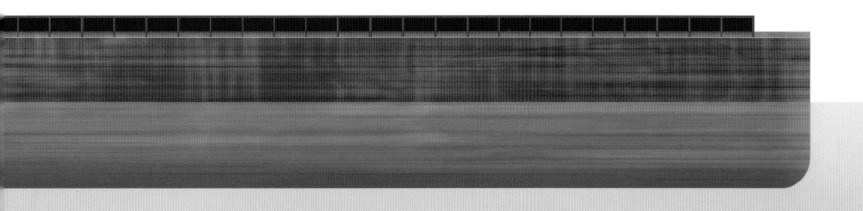

Does the Ark still exist and, if so, where is it and will we ever see it?

The Ark may be resting upon Mt. Ararat in Turkey, but so far, expeditions to find it have failed. The hope that it may still be on the mountain has been fueled by "sightings" over the years, such as an eyewitness account by a shepherd boy in 1905, or pilots in World War II who claimed to have seen the Ark as they flew over the mountain range. Whether it is lodged somewhere on the vast slopes of Ararat remains to be seen, but even if tangible evidence of its existence were found, it probably wouldn't change the minds of those who are skeptical of the Bible, anyway. Jesus himself said, "If they hear not Moses and the prophets, neither will they be persuaded, though one rose from the dead."

AUTHOR

*T*om Dooley is unquestionably one of the nation's top music-radio personalities. His stellar career spans more than 25 years with an impressive résumé of ratings successes at major market stations. Gifted with a voice made in heaven and a remarkable narrative ability, Tom Dooley is a top national "voice-over" talent. Tom began his career in Christian radio while at WFIL-Philadelphia in 1978 with a weekly Sunday morning show called "Alpha Omega." That program evolved over the years into what is now "The Journey," which Tom hosts six days a week from KVTT in Dallas, Texas. Along the way, he has been at some of the biggest stations in the country including WCBS-FM-New York, KHJ-Los Angeles, WFIL-Philadelphia, and KVIL-Dallas, where he still holds the record for midday ratings.

As national program director of CBN in Virginia Beach, he pioneered the nation's very first Christian music satellite radio network, Continental Radio. He has narrated countless documentaries, and his lists of commercials include clients like Radio Shack, Zales Jewelers, GE, and many more. Tom also served as the official "voice" of the Billy Graham Evangelistic Association, narrating many of Dr. Graham's national TV specials and several of his books on tape. Tom and his wife, Melanie, became born-again believers in Christ in 1977, and Tom became an ordained minister in 1996. They have been married 30 years and have three grown children. They live in Colleyville, Texas, with their boxers, Bugsy and Abby.

ILLUSTRATOR

$\mathcal{D}$allas-area illustrator Bill Looney is, to use the common vernacular, a "natural." He has painted commissioned portraits and artwork for scores of clients over the past three decades. He is a master of all art-related media including airbrush, oils, acrylics, computer illustration, and watercolor. Bill attended the University of Texas at Arlington and the Dallas Art Institute.

Bill honed his craft for many years in the demanding commercial world of graphic art design and illustration. A Christian since 1974, his desire to use his talents for the Lord led to his close friendship with Christian radio personality Tom Dooley. Having worked on several projects together, *The True Story of Noah's Ark* has been the most demanding and rewarding project so far. He is now employed full-time at MasterMedia working on future biblical productions.

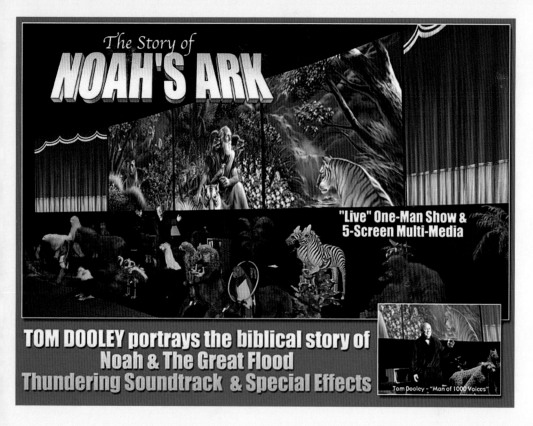

The Story of
NOAH'S ARK

"Live" One-Man Show &
5-Screen Multi-Media

TOM DOOLEY portrays the biblical story of
Noah & The Great Flood
Thundering Soundtrack & Special Effects

Tom Dooley - "Man of 1000 Voices"

THE STORY OF NOAH'S ARK has been produced into a two-hour stage production that synchronizes a "live" narrative by the author, Tom Dooley, with huge, animated, panoramic images across five gigantic screens — the same images seen in this book plus many more! It features a spectacular five-screen, multi-image presentation. This dynamic, high-energy, one-man show also features an exciting, original, musical soundtrack and the world's largest collection of authentic, life-size stuffed animals, two by two, of course. Special effects of fire, lighting, and thunder recreate the great Flood. See how amazingly different the world was when it was new before the Flood. *The Story of Noah's Ark* is educational, inspirational and very entertaining. For booking information call 1-800-343-7378. To see a video-demo online, visit: www.mastermedia.org.